KNOWiNG aND DoiNG WHaT'S RiGHT

The Positive Values Assets

by Pamela Espeland and Elizabeth Verdick

free spirit
PUBLiSHiNG®

Helping kids
help themselves™
since 1983

Library of Congress Cataloging-in-Publication Data
Espeland, Pamela.
    Knowing and doing what's right : the positive values assets / by Pamela Espeland and Elizabeth Verdick.
        p. cm.—(The adding assets series for kids; bk. 6)
    Includes index.
    ISBN-13: 978-1-57542-184-1
    ISBN-10: 1-57542-184-4
1. Children—Conduct of life. 2. Values—Juvenile literature. I. Verdick, Elizabeth. II. Title.
    BJ1631.E87 2006
    170′.44—dc22   2005027691

At the time of this book's publication, all facts and figures cited are the most current available; all tele- phone numbers, addresses, and Web site URLs are accurate and active; all publications, organizations, Web sites, and other resources exist as described in this book; and all have been verified. The author and Free Spirit Publishing make no warranty or guarantee concerning the information and materials given out by organizations or content found at Web sites, and we are not responsible for any changes that occur after this book's publication. If you find an error or believe that a resource listed here is not as described, please contact Free Spirit Publishing. Parents, teachers, and other adults: We strongly urge you to monitor children's use of the Internet.

Search Institute℠ and Developmental Assets™ are trademarks of Search Institute.

The original framework of 40 Developmental Assets (for adolescents) was developed by Search Institute © 1997, Minneapolis, MN 1-800-888-7828; *www.search-institute.org*. The Developmental Assets framework is used under license from Search Institute.

The FACTS! (pages 8, 22, 35, 47, 57, and 68) are from *Coming into Their Own: How Developmental Assets Promote Positive Growth in Middle Childhood* by Peter C. Scales, Arturo Sesma Jr., and Brent Bolstrom (Minneapolis: Search Institute, 2004).

Illustrated by Chris Sharp
Cover design by Marieka Heinlen
Interior design by Crysten Puszczykowski
Index by Ina Gravitz

10 9 8 7 6 5 4 3 2 1
Printed in the United States of America

Free Spirit Publishing Inc.
217 Fifth Avenue North, Suite 200
Minneapolis, MN 55401-1299
(612) 338-2068
help4kids@freespirit.com
www.freespirit.com

Free Spirit Publishing is a member of the Green Press Initiative, and we're committed to printing our books on recycled paper containing a minimum of 30% post consumer waste (PCW). For every ton of books printed on 30% PCW recycled paper, we save 5.1 trees, 2,100 gallons of water, 114 gallons of oil, 18 pounds of air pollution, 1,230 kilowatt hours of energy, and .9 cubic yards of landfill space. At Free Spirit it's our goal to nurture not only young people, but nature too!

Printed on recycled paper
including 30%
post-consumer waste

Contents

Introduction. 1

THE POSITIVE VALUES ASSETS

★ Caring 6

★ Equality and Social Justice. 20

★ Integrity 33

★ Honesty 45

★ Responsibility. 55

★ Healthy Lifestyle 66

A Note to Grown-ups 80

Helpful Resources 84

Index 88

About the Authors 91

Introduction

If you knew ways to make your life better, right now and for the future, would you try them?

We're guessing you would, and that's why we wrote this book. It's part of a series of eight books called the **Adding Assets Series for Kids.**

What Are Assets, Anyway?

When we use the word **assets**, we mean good things you need in your life and yourself.

We don't mean houses, cars, property, and jewelry—assets whose value is measured in money. We mean **Developmental Assets** that help you to be and become your best. Things like a close, loving family. A neighborhood where you feel safe. Adults you look up to and respect. And (sorry!) doing your homework.

There are 40 Developmental Assets in all. This book is about adding six of them to your life. They're called the **Positive Values Assets** because they're about the beliefs that guide your choices and behaviors. Some people might call these your *morals.* Other people might call them your *conscience.* Positive values keep you from doing things you shouldn't do, even when you really want to do them. And they give you the inner strength to do things you should do, even when it's risky or hard. Your values show the world what kind of person you are. When you have positive values, you care about others—and you respect yourself.

The Positive Values Assets

Asset Name	What It Means
Caring	Your parent(s) tell you it's important to help other people.
Equality and Social Justice	Your parent(s) tell you it's important to speak up for equal rights for all people.
Integrity	Your parent(s) tell you it's important to stand up for your beliefs.
Honesty	Your parent(s) tell you it's important to be truthful.
Responsibility	Your parent(s) tell you it's important to be responsible for your own behavior.
Healthy Lifestyle	Your parent(s) tell you it's important to have good health habits and an understanding of healthy sexuality.

Other books in the series are about the other 34 assets.* That may seem like a lot, but don't worry. You don't have to add them all at once. You don't have to

---

* If you're curious to know what the other assets are, you can read the whole list on pages 82–83.

add them in any particular order. But the sooner you can add them to your life, the better.

Why You Need Assets

An organization called Search Institute surveyed hundreds of thousands of kids and teens across the United States. Their researchers found that some kids have a fairly easy time growing up, while others don't. Some kids get involved in harmful behaviors or dangerous activities, while others don't.

What makes the difference? Developmental Assets! Kids who have them are more likely to do well. Kids who don't have them are less likely to do well.

Maybe you're thinking, "Why should I have to add my own assets? I'm just a kid!" Because kids have the power to make choices in their lives. You can choose to sit back and wait for other people to help you, or you can choose to help yourself. You can also work with other people who care about you and want to help.

Many of the ideas in this book involve working with other people—like your parents, grandparents, aunts, uncles, and other family grown-ups. And your teachers, neighbors, coaches, Scout leaders, and religious leaders. They can all help add assets for you and with you.

It's likely that many of the adults in your life are already helping. In fact, an adult probably gave you this book to read.

How to Use This Book

Start by choosing **one** asset to add. Read the stories at the beginning and end of that chapter. The stories are examples of the assets in everyday life. Then pick **one** idea and try it. See how it goes. After that, try another idea, or move on to another asset.

Don't worry about being perfect or getting it right. Know that by trying, you're doing something great for yourself.

The more assets you add, the better you'll feel about yourself and your future. Soon you won't be a kid anymore. You'll be a teenager. Because you have assets, you'll feel and be a lot more sure of yourself. You'll make better decisions. You'll have a head start on success.

We wish you the very best as you add assets to your life.

Pamela Espeland and Elizabeth Verdick
Minneapolis, MN

A Few Words About Families

Kids today live in many different kinds of families.

Maybe you live with one or both of your parents. Maybe you live with other adult relatives—aunts and uncles, grandparents, grown-up brothers or sisters or cousins.

Maybe you live with a stepparent, foster parent, or guardian. Maybe you live with one of your parents and his or her life partner.

In this series, we use the word **parents** to describe the adults who care for you in your home. We also use **family adults, family grown-ups,** and **adults at home.** When you see any of these words, think of your own family, whatever kind it is.

Caring

Hanna & Tim's Story

"Tell us all about the senior center, Tim," says Mom as she braids Hanna's hair.

Tim gives one of Hanna's braids a playful tug. "You should have been there, Hanna. You're good at games like bingo. You would've had fun. I got to turn the bingo ball—Mr. Gerard let me!"

"No fair!" Hanna says, turning to look at her older brother.

"Well, you could have come," Tim replies. "I've invited you about a hundred times."

Hanna turns back around in a huff and flips her braids over her shoulder.

"Hey, it's Pippi Longstocking," Tim says, laughing.

"Ha, ha. You're a dork," says Hanna.

"Well, you're a big baby. You're scared of old people."

"Am not!" Hanna says loudly, but she knows she's not fooling anyone. She *is* scared of the people at the senior center.

"Okay, please cut it out, you two," Mom warns. "Tim, can you go feed Fat Cat? He's waiting by his dish."

After Tim leaves, Mom says, "You know, Hanna, I think I understand your fear. You haven't been around many elderly people. Tim teases you, but deep down, he really wants you to come along so you can volunteer with him. He cares about a lot of those folks, and he wants to introduce you to them."

Hanna sighs. "But, Mom, I feel sorry for them! Some of them are sick. Some of them are all alone, and no one in their family comes to visit them—Tim said so!"

Mom puts her arm around Hanna and pulls her close. "Isn't that all the more reason to go with Tim sometime? Will you think about it at least?"

"Yeah, I'll think about it. I promise."

Tim has the *Caring* asset, and he wants his sister to have it, too.

Think about your own life. Do you believe it's important to help others? Do you care about people besides your own family and friends? Has a family adult talked to you about ways to show other people you care?

If **YES**, keep reading to learn ways to make this asset even stronger.

> ## Facts!
>
> **Kids with the *Caring* asset:**
>
> ✓ are more likely to help others in need
>
> ✓ do better in school
>
> ✓ are less *agressive* (pushy and violent)

If **NO**, keep reading to learn ways to add this asset to your life.

You can also use these ideas to help add this asset for other people—like your friends, family members, neighbors, and kids at school.

ways to Add This Asset

 **AT HOME**

Think About What Your Parents Have Taught You. Has your mom or dad told you it's important to care about other people and not just yourself? Do other adults in your family tell you this, too? Or maybe they show by example how to be kind and loving. What do they do? How do they help other people? Today, thank one of the adults in your family for teaching you about caring. (This is a great way to show *you* care.)

Walk in Someone Else's Shoes. Have you ever heard the expression "Put yourself in my shoes"? It's not about wearing someone else's stinky sneakers! It's about imagining how it might feel to be another person—to think their thoughts, have their feelings, and live their day-to-day life. Whose "shoes" might you wear for a little while today? Your stepmom's? Your little brother's? Your grandpa's? What might life look like from this person's point of view? What makes this person feel happy, sad, lonely, or excited? Use your imagination to see your family in a more caring light.

> **Tip:** Walking in someone else's shoes builds *empathy*—the ability to understand how other people feel. The more empathy you have for others, the more you realize that people aren't all that different, and the easier it is to be a caring person.

Show You Care Every Day. Doing something kind for someone else is a win-win act. First, you make the other person feel good. And second, *you* feel good inside. What are some ways you might be nicer to each person in your family? Could you do a chore without being asked? Or invite your sister to join in

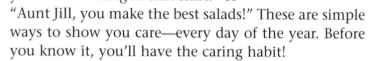

when you've got a friend over? Could you write letters or emails to relatives who want to hear from you more often? How about giving people compliments like, "Dad, you look amazing in that shirt!" or "Aunt Jill, you make the best salads!" These are simple ways to show you care—every day of the year. Before you know it, you'll have the caring habit!

Go Further. Caring is about helping other people. That includes people outside your family, like your neighbors, classmates, people in your community (whether you know them or not), and even people in faraway countries. What are some ways your family shows they care about people? Do you volunteer together? Do you donate money, food, clothing, or other items to people in need? Do you ever participate in fundraising activities, like walkathons or community bake sales? Do you help out whenever you see that someone could use a hand? If your family already has this asset, that's great. Keep it up! But if you think your family could spend more time caring for others, *you* could be the one to suggest it. You might say something like, "Grandma, let's go make a donation to an animal shelter." Or you could ask to have a family meeting so you can talk about this asset together and brainstorm ways to help others.

Get Past Anything That's Holding You Back. Maybe you've thought about volunteering to help people, but you haven't actually started because you feel nervous or a little bit scared. It's natural for some kids to worry about what it might be like to talk to elderly people, feed homeless families at a shelter, or play with young children who have special needs. You might wonder if you'll end up feeling sad or if something unexpected might happen. But that doesn't have to stop you from reaching out to people who need your help. You *can* do it—and you'll probably feel really good that you did. Talk to a family grown-up about any fears or concerns you might have.

TIP: If another family member comes with you to lend a hand, you'll probably feel more confident and less anxious.

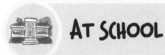

AT SCHOOL

★ Caring for others includes being of service to them. And being of service means offering your help on a project or just spending time with someone in need. Your school probably has a service club you could join. When you're in a service club, you learn that it's cool to care. You get to join up with other students who take pride in helping and want to do their part to make the world a kinder, more caring place. Today, take one step toward learning more about your school's service club.

★ What if your school doesn't have a service club? Talk with your teacher about starting or getting your class involved in a project designed to help others. Need ideas? How about getting your class (or your whole grade) to make cards for elderly people at a retirement center? Or collecting school supplies for kids who aren't able to afford them? Or gathering donated suitcases and duffle bags for kids in foster care?

Places to Go for Inspiration

Use a computer at school to visit these Web sites and read about caring people.

★ The Giraffe Heroes Project. Read stories about Giraffe Heroes—people who stick their necks out for the common good. Check out the For Kids Only section of the site. *www.giraffe.org*

★ Points of Light Foundation. Each weekday, one volunteer or group receives a Point of Light Award. Search the Web site for "Daily

Points of Light" to read stories reaching back to 1998. (That's thousands of stories!) You can even search for award winners in your city and state. *www.pointsoflight.org*

Take a trip to your local library and look for this book.

★ *Kids' Random Acts of Kindness* (Berkeley, CA: Conari Press, 1994). Children from around the world tell their own stories of kindness and caring toward others.

IN YOUR NEIGHBORHOOD

★ Good neighbors know lots of ways to show they care. They might lend each other tools, bring over home-baked goodies to share, or offer to care for each other's pets when needed. But these sorts of actions aren't only for grown-ups. Kids can show they care, too. How? Pretty much in the same ways adults do. You could lend a neighbor kid some of your books, make a dozen cookies to share, or offer to feed someone's fish or hamster if the family plans to be away for a few days.

★ Ask a family grown-up about people in your neighborhood who might need special help. *Examples:* Is there a single parent raising a young child? (Maybe you could be a parent's helper for an hour or two per week). An elderly person who no longer drives? (Maybe you and your family could take the person to the grocery store once a week.) A child your age who seems lonely? (Try to make friends.) Brainstorm other ways to help.

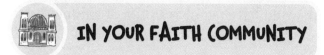

IN YOUR FAITH COMMUNITY

★ Nearly all faith communities focus on caring for and helping others. Maybe you've heard the message so many times during services or youth group meetings that you aren't really listening. If that's true, make a special effort to tune back in. Think about ways you've helped others or how others have helped you. Listen to the stories of people who have acted unselfishly or reached out to those in need. Remember those lessons—and do your part to help others in your faith community, too.

Ask About Starting a Kids Care Club

A Kids Care Club is a group of young people who work together to help others in their community and around the world. Clubs are formed in schools, faith communities, volunteer centers, and with organizations such as scout troops and 4-H clubs. You have to be 18 or older to start a club, so this is something you'll need to talk about with a religious leader, teacher, youth group leader, or another grown-up. Ask the adult to visit the Kids Care Clubs Web site (*www.kidscare.org*). Ask what you can do to get the ball rolling.

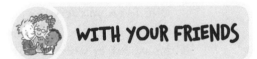

WITH YOUR FRIENDS

★ Do your friends know how much you care about them? Maybe they do . . . or maybe you only think they do. It's okay to be more obvious about how much you care. Give more hugs or high fives. Offer compliments like, "You tell the best jokes!" Do favors for your friends (and notice when they do favors for you). Say, "I'm really glad you're my friend" every once in a while.

⭐ Volunteering with your best friend can be more fun than volunteering on your own. The two of you can start at home by donating items to a charitable organization you both care about. Go through your drawers and closets to look for clothing, shoes, and toys you've outgrown. Make sure all are clean and in excellent condition, then pack them up in boxes and bags.

> **TIP:** Invite your parents to look over what you'd like to donate and to help you get the items to a drop-off center.

Start Adding!

Pick at least ONE idea you've read here and give it a try. Then think about or write about what happened. Will you try another way to become a more caring person and help others?

Back to
Hanna &
Tim's
Story

A week later, Fat Cat sits in his kitty carrier in the backseat of the car, between Hanna and Tim.

"This was such a great idea, Hanna!" Tim says. "All the residents are going to love Fat Cat. I'm glad Mr. Gerard is letting us do this."

Hanna smiles, even though she's nervous.

At the senior center, Mom says, "Okay, I'll be back in an hour to pick you up. Enjoy yourselves!" As she bends down to hug Hanna, Mom whispers, "I'm proud of you."

Mr. Gerard comes out to greet them. He shakes Hanna's hand and peeks into the carrier Tim is holding. "So this must be the famous Fat Cat. I see he lives up to his name," he says, smiling.

Inside the center, Hanna is full of curiosity. She looks around and sees residents reading, doing crafts, watching TV, and talking.

"Can we go visit Mrs. Brooks first?" Tim asks.

Mr. Gerard says, "Sure thing. Last I checked, she was in her room."

On the way, Mr. Gerard gives Hanna a tour. "We have a nice cafeteria. You probably smell lunch cooking—I know I do. And down that hallway, past where you can see right now, is the exercise room."

"Old people *exercise?*" Hanna says in surprise. She quickly feels embarrassed. "Oh! I didn't mean to say that. Sorry!"

Tim rolls his eyes. "She has some crazy ideas about stuff," he says to Mr. Gerard.

"No need to explain," he says kindly. "Well, here we are! I'll check back later."

Mrs. Brooks looks up, sees Tim, and smiles. "Well, if it isn't my favorite young man! And I see you've brought company."

"My sister, Hanna, and our cat," Tim replies. He sets down the carrier and takes Fat Cat out.

Mrs. Brooks pats the chair beside her and says to Hanna, "Come, sit. Let's get to know each other. And bring that sweet kitty over, won't you?"

Hanna notices a bunch of photos around the room, some in color, others in black and white.

"See that photo over there?" Mrs. Brooks asks Hanna, while gently petting the cat. "My older brother, Frank. He was a rascal. Teased me all the time!"

"Then we have something in common!" Hanna exclaims.

"Oh, *really?*" Mrs. Brooks asks. She says under her breath so only Hanna can hear, "Then I'll bet you could use some good comebacks. I've got a bunch of them!"

Hanna whispers, "Do you think I could stop by later when Tim's not here so you can tell me?"

"Absolutely!"

"What are you two whispering about?" Tim asks.

"Nothing!" Hanna and Mrs. Brooks say at the exact same time. Then they both start laughing. Hanna realizes that she feels really glad to be there.

Equality and Social Justice

What it means: Your parent(s) tell you it's important to speak up for equal rights for all people.

Kia's Story Kia listens as the other kids in her class take turns reading from the Language Arts textbook. She scans down to the next paragraph, looking it over. "Oh, no," she thinks, realizing that Isaac's turn is next. "He's got a long paragraph with a bunch of hard words."

"Isaac, your turn," the teacher says.

Isaac stumbles over the first sentence. He starts over. Each word comes out slowly, and Kia hears the other kids start to snicker, like they always do. After what seems like forever, Isaac finishes the paragraph.

"Thank you," their teacher says. "Kia, you're next." Kia tries not to read her paragraph too fast because she doesn't want to make Isaac look worse.

Later, while everyone's standing around their lockers, Kia hears Ben and his friends laughing about Isaac. One of them says, "He's so retarded!"

Kia slams her locker door and turns to the group. If there's one thing she can't stand, it's when people use that word lightly.

"I can't believe you guys act this way," she says. "People come to school to learn, you know. And it's not easy to learn when you're being laughed at."

"Sorry, Miss Goody-Goody!" Ben says with a smirk. "Are you going to send me to the principal?" Kia gives him a look and heads down the hall. Isaac follows her.

"Wait up, Kia! I have something to say."

She stops and faces Isaac, who looks angry. "I can fight my own battles, Kia."

"What?" she asks, surprised.

"I don't need you to try to pro- tect me like I'm some little kid."

"But I just thought—"

"Let them laugh. So what if I'm not perfect at reading?"

"But they shouldn't treat people—"

"Kia, I can take care of myself!" Isaac says. He turns and walks away.

She stares after him, feeling confused.

Kia has the *Equality and Social Justice* asset. But sometimes she's totally mixed up about the way people act.

Think about your own life. Have you been taught that all people are equal? Do the adults in your family talk to you about showing respect to others? Have you learned that all people have the right to be treated with fairness?

If **YES**, keep reading to learn ways to make this asset even stronger.

If **NO**, keep reading to learn ways to add this asset to your life.

> ## Facts!
>
> **Kids with the *Equality and Social Justice* asset:**
>
> ✔ **get better grades in school**
>
> ✔ **have more *empathy* for others (the ability to understand how other people feel)**
>
> ✔ **have higher self-esteem**

You can also use these ideas to help add this asset for other people—like your friends, family members, neighbors, and kids at school.

ways to Add This Asset

 **AT HOME**

Make an "I Believe . . ." List. You've probably heard the word *values* before. (All of the assets in this book are about positive values.) What are *your* values—the things in life you believe to be true and are willing to stand up for? What are the ideas that guide your behavior, how you treat yourself, and how you treat others? Maybe you value getting a good education, telling the truth, being kind, or all of the above. Those are some really positive values! Have you ever put your values into writing? You might make a list of them now. Start by writing "I believe . . ." at the top of a piece of paper, then add 5–10 values you want to live by. *Examples:* "I believe that animals deserve to be treated with kindness. I believe that families are important. I believe that it's wrong to make fun of people." When you see your values written down, they'll seem more real and worth striving for every day. Decorate your list, if you'd like. Hang it on a wall or bulletin board so you can look at it often.

The Universal Declaration of Human Rights

Do you believe that all human beings are born free and we should all be treated in the same way? That everyone has the right to live in freedom and safety? That no one should be arrested without a good reason?

These are all *articles* (sections) within the Universal Declaration of Human Rights. It was adopted by the General Assembly of the United Nations on December 10, 1948. Because of the Declaration, people around the world know what human rights are. Look for a copy in your school's media center, your local library, or on the Web. Many Web sites have it available to read online or download. Here's one:

Universal Declaration of Human Rights 50th Anniversary
www.udhr.org

Find Out Your Family's Values. The grown-ups in your family probably have values of their own. Do they talk to you about them? Yes, no, or hardly ever? Many families are so busy that they forget to talk about values and beliefs. But there's no law that says *you* can't start the conversation. You might ask, "What are some of the values that are really important for us?" The adults in your family might be inspired by a question like that, and it could be the start of a really interesting talk.

Learn About Social Justice. What is *social justice*, anyway? Here's one definition: "The belief in a fair, compassionate world where differences are understood and valued, and where human dignity, the Earth, our ancestors, and future generations are respected." Here's another definition: "Social justice is about preventing human rights abuses and ensuring that people obey international law." Talk with your family and other trusted adults about social justice. See if you can come up with your own definition. Write it down.

Appreciate Your Freedoms. You probably have a lot of freedoms you take for granted. *Examples:* You might naturally expect that one day you'll get your driver's license, earn your high-school diploma, vote in your first election, and become whatever you want to be when you're an adult. Did you know that not all kids grow up free to do those things? Maybe you never thought about how many freedoms you have, especially since you're still young and you have a lot of adult rules to follow (like having to go to school or having a bedtime). Sure, you've got rules to deal with, but you also have some amazing rights and freedoms. Think about them . . . talk about them . . . learn about them and the people who made them possible. You may feel a new respect for how lucky you are.

Take a Look at What You *Really* Feel. Do you truly believe that everyone is born equal? Or do you sometimes feel that certain people are worse (or better) than others because of their ethnic background, skin color, where they live, religious beliefs, or how much money their family seems to have? Have you ever labeled anyone (out loud or to yourself) a "geek," a "goody-goody," or a term having to do with his or her race or religion? There's probably not a single person in the world who hasn't labeled someone else at least once, so you're not alone if you said yes to one or more of these questions. Depending on what your family has taught you, you may have strong feelings about whether all people are born equal or not. Now that you're learning about the Equality and Social Justice asset, how are your views changing?

Write in Your Journal. Have you ever been called a hurtful name because of your *gender* (being a girl or boy), race, religion, looks, age, or where you live? If you have, how did you react? Did you feel angry? Sad? Shocked? Confused? A mix of feelings? Did you wonder how someone could say such a thing about you? Did you tell the person it wasn't fair or true, or did you keep your feelings to yourself? Did you believe or reject what the person said? Write in your journal about what happened. Be honest about the feelings that came up then (and may still come up now). What did you learn about yourself? What did you learn about equality, social justice, and fairness?

 **AT SCHOOL**

★ Bullying is a problem at every school—how about yours? Are there students who pick on kids who are smaller or seem weaker? Do some kids tease others about their looks, clothes, or skills? Bullies rarely believe in equality and social justice. They like feeling powerful over others. You don't have to take what a bully dishes out—and you don't have to stand on the sidelines while someone else is being hurt or harassed. Stand up for yourself and others by telling your teachers and principal about what happens in the hallways and on the playground. You have the right to be safe at school.

★ Make a promise to yourself not to tease people in class, during recess, or on the bus. Refuse to join in when others are teasing. You might say, "That's not cool, and I don't want to be a part of it." Then walk away. If you've teased someone in the past, you could apologize—today. It may not feel comfortable, but if you just go up and say you're sorry, you'll feel better afterward (and so might the person you teased).

IN YOUR NEIGHBORHOOD

★ Look out for younger kids who get picked on, teased, or bullied. Stand up for them when it's safe for you to do so, or help make them feel better once the bully has left. You could say something like, "Don't let that kid bother you. I think you're really cool."

★ Get to know kids in your neighborhood who aren't just like you. If you're a boy, you can have friends who are girls . . . and if you're a girl, you can have friends who are boys. You can have friends who are older or younger than you, or friends who come from a different racial or ethnic background.

IN YOUR FAITH COMMUNITY

★ Talk with your youth leader about joining forces with other youth groups to work on an equality and social justice issue. *Examples:* You could all get involved in a food drive, or a community-wide anti-bullying campaign. You'll get to know kids of a different faith while doing something positive for others.

Be an AI Kid

Maybe you've heard about Amnesty International (AI), an organization that works for human rights around the world. Through AI, kids can make a difference by writing letters to public officials about Prisoners of Conscience (POCs). POCs are non-violent people who have been jailed by a government for political reasons. Kids can also write postcards to POCs to help cheer them up. Want to know more? Visit the AIKids part of AI's Web site. Learn about AI and human rights, download a letter-writing guide, and try some games and activities for kids. This might be a great project for your religious education class or youth group.

AIKids
www.amnestyusa.org/aikids

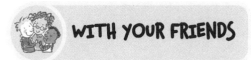

WITH YOUR FRIENDS

⭐ Friendship is much more than hanging out together and having a good time (although those things are important, too). Being a true friend also includes standing by your friends and sticking up for them in the toughest social situations. Next time a friend of yours is bullied or teased, don't be a silent witness. Tell the bullies or teasers that you don't like what they're doing and that you and your friend won't put up with it.

Start Adding!

Pick at least ONE idea you've read here and give it a try. Then think about or write about what happened. Will you try another idea to show what you know and believe about equality and social justice?

Back to
Kia's
Story
At dinner, Kia picks at her food.

"Lasagna is your favorite. Aren't you hungry?" her dad asks.

"No. I mean, yes. I mean, something happened at school today."

"What was it?" her mom asks.

Kia puts down her fork. "There's this kid named Isaac. You've seen him at school, Mom. He's got red hair, and he's really tall?"

"Yes, I know him," Kia's mom says.

"Well, the other kids tease him because he can't read very well, and I hate it! It's not fair."

"You're right, it's not," says her dad. "Unfortunately, teasing happens. I wish it didn't."

"Yeah, and kids call people 'retard' or 'feeb' and stuff like that!" Kia says angrily. "It really upsets me. You know, partly because of McKenna."

Her little sister, McKenna, has already finished dinner and is now in the family room, playing with her dolls and singing a made-up song.

Kia sees her parents look at each other with concern. Mom lets out a breath and says, "I don't like it when people who have disabilities get teased, either. It's just not right."

"And we worry about McKenna, like you do, Kia," says her dad. "The best that all of us can do is stand up for her, and stand by her."

"I know. It's what you keep telling me. But Mom, Dad, I *did* try to stand up for Isaac today, and he got mad at me for it."

"What do you mean?" asks Dad.

"He told me he can fight his own battles."

"Hmmm," says her mom. "Well, I suppose he has a point there. One day, we hope McKenna will be able to stand up for herself if she has to. But Kia, today you were just doing what you thought was right."

"That's true," Dad adds. "And we're proud of you for knowing that all people deserve respect."

Kia feels a little better.

Then her mom says quietly, "Life sure can be complicated, can't it?"

Integrity

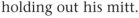

Adam's Story

"Adam, I can't wait for your party. The arcade totally rocks!" says Ricardo, tossing the baseball to Adam.

Adam catches the ball in his mitt and throws it back. "Yeah, it's going to be fun. Did your dad say it's okay?"

"Yeah, I'm in. So, how many guys are going?"

Adam throws a slider. "Five. And Ellie."

Ricardo leaps to catch the ball. "Ellie?" he says, looking disappointed.

"Yeah, Ellie." Adam asks. "Here, toss it," he says, holding out his mitt.

Ricardo keeps hold of the ball. "Dude, she's a girl."

"So? What's the problem?"

"Aren't you just inviting the guys?" Ricardo looks down at the ball, pauses, and finally throws it again.

Adam makes a quick catch and chucks it back. "Well, Ellie's my neighbor. And she's really nice. We've been friends since kindergarten."

Ricardo starts lobbing the ball in the air above him and catching it repeatedly. "We'll have way more fun without her. Girls hate video games. They're no good at them, anyway."

"Uh, you've never seen Ellie play, then," Adam says, getting annoyed.

"When I had my party, I didn't invite any girls."

"Ricardo, would you throw me the ball? It's *my* party, not yours. Besides, I promised Ellie."

"All I'm saying is it's lame to invite a girl."

"Ricardo, Ellie's my friend. And I'm *not* going to un-invite her."

Adam knows that having the *Integrity* asset means keeping your promises and standing up for your beliefs.

Think about your own life. Has a parent or another adult in your family talked to you about your values and beliefs? Do you stand up for what you believe in? (Do you *know* what you believe in?) Do you keep your promises to other people—and to yourself?

If **YES,** keep reading to learn ways to make this asset even stronger.

> ## Facts!
>
> **Kids with the *Integrity* asset:**
>
> ✓ see themselves as more capable
>
> ✓ have fewer behavior problems
>
> ✓ feel more hopeful

If **NO,** keep reading to learn ways to add this asset to your life.

You can also use these ideas to help add this asset for other people—like your friends, family members, neighbors, and kids at school.

AT HOME

Stand Strong. Having beliefs is important—but you can't just stop there. You've also got to *stand by* those beliefs when they're tested and *stand up for them* if needed. *Example:* Maybe you believe in being loyal to your friends. But what if your loyalty is tested?

For instance, suppose a friend is cranky at lunch. She spills your milk without apologizing, then says she hates what you're wearing. Do you (A) refuse to talk to her for the rest of the day or (B) ask her what's up and tell her, kindly, that she's hurting your feelings? A loyal friend would choose (B). *X-treme example:* Later, another friend who saw what happened at lunch says, "She is so rude—let's ignore her during recess." In a case like this, you'd be standing up for your beliefs if you stuck by *both* friends. How do you do that? By saying something like, "I've got a better idea. Let's all play together. It will be more fun that way."

Find Integrity Role Models. Integrity means matching your actions to your beliefs. Maybe you've heard about an African American civil rights hero named Rosa Parks. She refused to give up her seat on a public bus to a white man, even though that's what African-Americans in Alabama were supposed to do in the 1950s. Her choice wasn't easy—and it certainly wasn't popular at the time. She showed integrity (and courage, too). Not all of us will take a stand quite like that, but many of us take smaller steps that show our integrity. What about the adults in your family? How do they show integrity? What has this taught you? How might you follow in the footsteps of your family role models?

Picture Yourself Positively. Do you think of yourself as honest, caring, fair, and rich in integrity? You should! You have many positive qualities that you can keep building on every day. One fun way to express all the new things you're learning about yourself is to make a self-portrait showing the assets you have.

Ask a family member to take your picture, or just draw a picture of yourself. Mount your self-portrait on a piece of cardboard or poster board. Around this image, write words or phrases that describe who you are and what you believe. *Examples:* *Honesty, I keep my promises, Strength, Purpose, Values, I have integrity, Do the right thing, Believe.* You can even glue on symbols that have meaning to you, creating a collage. How about a peace sign, a special message from a fortune cookie, a friendship bracelet, or a kind note that someone wrote about you?

TIP: You can turn this into an activity for your whole family. Instead of a self-portrait, use a family photo. Work together to add words and symbols that have special meaning for everyone.

Check It Out

You and your family might want to look in the library for this book:

★ *What Do You Stand For? For Kids: A Guide to Building Character* by Barbara A. Lewis (Minneapolis: Free Spirit Publishing, 2005).

You'll learn a lot about positive values and character traits like caring, honesty, responsibility, and more. Together, you can read the true stories and try the activities.

If there are older kids in your family, look for this book:

★ *What Do You Stand For? For Teens: A Guide to Building Character* by Barbara A. Lewis (Minneapolis: Free Spirit Publishing, 2005).

 AT SCHOOL

★ In school, have you learned about Rosa Parks, Martin Luther King Jr., Mother Teresa, Gandhi, Abraham Lincoln, or other people who were known for their integrity (and many other amazing qualities as well)? Ask your teacher or school librarian for tips on finding more information about these heroes in books or online. Discover what these famous figures stood for and the brave things they did to live by their beliefs. Share what you've learned with the other kids in your class.

★ Look around you at school: Who shows integrity? Are there some kids in your class who take pride in being honest, acting fair, or refusing to cheat? If so, can these students be role models for you? And what about the adults at your school—teachers, your principal, office workers, aides, and so on? Which ones seem to have integrity, and how can you tell? See if your teacher would be willing to work with you and other students to create a bulletin board with examples of people who show integrity. You can include the famous and the not-yet-famous (like the people you see every day at school).

IN YOUR NEIGHBORHOOD

★ You probably know some older adults in your apartment building or neighborhood. With age comes wisdom, or so it's been said. Talk to these neighbors about what you've learned about integrity and see what they have to say. Ask about their heroes and role models. Sometimes, talking with someone who's much older than you can be an eye-opening experience.

★ Notice when younger children show integrity. Although younger kids may not yet know what the word *integrity* means, they do sometimes act in ways that are honest, fair, and right. When it happens, point it out and praise them.

 IN YOUR FAITH COMMUNITY

★ Ask your religious leader or youth group leader to make "integrity" the focus of services one day. What does your faith teach you about being a person with integrity? Share what you've been learning about the topic, if you feel comfortable doing so. On that same day, or as a follow-up, talk about what happens when people don't show integrity. *Examples:* What are the consequences of lying, cheating, or not standing up for your beliefs? Who gets hurt (besides you) and why?

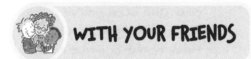 WITH YOUR FRIENDS

★ Look at the "Picture Yourself Positively" activity on page 37. Try it with a friend! You can either help your friend make his or her own self-portrait, or you can create one together using a photo of the two of you.

★ This may not be easy, but if a friend does something that goes against his or her values (or yours), speak up. *Example:* If your friend writes in a library book or asks to copy off your math quiz, say something about it. You could try, "Hey, that's not something you'd usually do—what's up?" or "Sorry, but I'm not comfortable with that."

Start Adding!

Pick at least ONE idea you've read here and give it a try. Then think about or write about what happened. Will you try another idea to build your integrity and to help others stand up for their beliefs?

Back to
Adam's
Story
Ricardo takes off his baseball mitt and throws it on the ground.

"Are you mad or something?" Adam asks.

"Yeah, you're not listening to me about the arcade! I don't even like Ellie. She called me 'pig-headed.'"

Adam laughs. "I wonder where she got that idea."

Adam's stepmom, Carol, calls them in, saying, "Ricardo, your grandpa's here to pick you up!"

The boys go inside, barely looking at each other. Ricardo doesn't even say good-bye.

"Fine, if that's the way you want to be about it," Adam mutters. He flings open the refrigerator door and grabs a bottle of water.

"Did something happen?" his stepmom asks.

"Me and Ricardo had a stupid fight."

"Can I ask what about?"

"He was getting all weird about Ellie coming to my birthday party," Adam replies.

"I don't get it," Carol says.

"Neither do I. He's saying it won't be fun with a girl there."

"Well, this isn't the first time Ricardo's acted stubborn about something."

"Yeah, I know," he admits. "But he's still my friend."

"He is," Carol says. "And so is Ellie."

Adam opens the water bottle and takes a big gulp. "You know what?" he says. "I'm not going to let Ricardo get me down. I'm going to have fun at my party, no matter what."

Carol smiles. "Adam, I admire your integrity."

"What's that mean?" he asks.

She kisses him on the cheek. "Let's just say it means I think you're pretty cool."

Honesty

What it means: Your parent(s) tell you it's important to be truthful.

Brianna's Story

"Okay, I finished, Daddy!" Brianna calls out. "My room's all clean. Can I go outside now?"

"You made your bed?"

"Yep."

"You put your clothes away?"

"Uh-huh."

"Desk?"

"Yes! I did everything on my list of Saturday chores. My friends are waiting for me."

"Okay, you're good to go. Have fun!"

Brianna runs outdoors into the sunshine and heads for the park. Her friends are already at the basketball court, warming up. "Did you choose teams yet?" she asks.

45

"Nope, we waited for you," says her best friend, Nadia. "You and I get to be team captains today."

Brianna can't wait to get out on the court and try some of her moves. But her mood changes quickly when she sees her dad in the distance, walking toward them.

"Brianna, what's up?" Nadia asks quietly. "Your father looks mad."

"Oh, no! I lied to him about getting my chores done!" says Brianna. She thinks about the mess on her desk that she was hoping her dad wouldn't notice. And the clean laundry she left on her bed instead of putting away. And the closet . . . where she'd tossed everything that had been on the floor, including her breakfast dishes.

"Hello, girls," her dad says, a serious expression on his face. "I'm sorry, but Brianna won't be playing any basketball today—or the rest of the weekend."

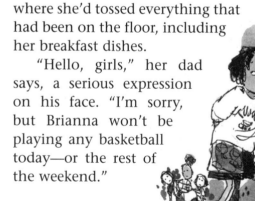

Brianna needs to work on the *Honesty* asset.

Think about your own life. Has a parent or another family adult talked to you about the importance of telling the truth? Do you try to be honest all (or most of) the time? Even when it's not easy? When you tell a lie, do you admit it and try to make things right?

If **YES,** keep reading to learn ways to make this asset even stronger.

If **NO,** keep reading to learn ways to add this asset to your life.

Facts!

Kids with the *Honesty* **asset:**

✓ worry less about school

✓ are better at resolving conflicts

✓ have a stronger sense of well-being

You can also use these ideas to help add this asset for other people—like your friends, family members, neighbors, and kids at school.

AT HOME

Be Honest with Your Family. Some lies are easy to tell and get away with, like "Yeah, Mom, I brushed my teeth for two minutes, want to smell my breath?" In fact, you may hardly think twice about little lies like that because they don't seem to hurt anyone. Or do they? Think about it for a minute. The lie might get your mom off your case, and you might get away with not brushing your teeth for as long as she wanted you to. But you could end up with some bad habits (and not just ones that affect your teeth). *Examples:* You might lie to your mom about other things you haven't done. Or you might get caught in a lie, then end up lying even more to cover up your first lie. You know the old saying, "Honesty is the best policy." Well, it's true!

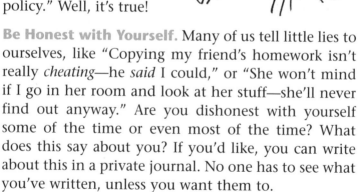

Be Honest with Yourself. Many of us tell little lies to ourselves, like "Copying my friend's homework isn't really *cheating*—he *said* I could," or "She won't mind if I go in her room and look at her stuff—she'll never find out anyway." Are you dishonest with yourself some of the time or even most of the time? What does this say about you? If you'd like, you can write about this in a private journal. No one has to see what you've written, unless you want them to.

Commit to the Truth. Have a family meeting to talk about honesty. What are your family's rules about telling the truth? What happens when family members break those rules? Are the consequences different for grown-ups and kids? See if everyone can admit to a time when they lied and how it felt. What would each person do differently if given the chance to relive that moment? Talk about the differences between big lies and small ones. Is it ever okay to lie? Why or why not? Write a family pledge to be honest and truthful, even when it's not easy.

5 Terrific Reasons to Tell the Truth

1. It shows that you're honest and trustworthy.

2. It proves that you have values you live by.

3. It helps people know what *really* happened—so no one will be unfairly blamed.

4. It's easier! You won't have to keep your story straight (because it's not a story, it's the truth). And you won't have to tell new lies to cover up old ones.

5. It helps you feel more positive and confident—and it inspires others to tell the truth, too.

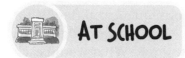

AT SCHOOL

★ Get everyone involved in making a classroom poster or bulletin board about honesty. You might start with "5 Terrific Reasons to Tell the Truth" on page 49 or come up with your own words.

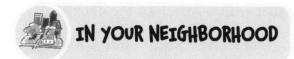

IN YOUR NEIGHBORHOOD

★ Be honest when you play games and sports. Don't say, "I tagged you!" when you didn't, or "That was out of bounds!" when it wasn't. Sure, you want to win, but wouldn't you rather win fair and square, without lying or cheating? If other kids bend the rules or try to get away with lies, call them on it.

★ If you accidentally break your friend's video game, admit it. If you crash your bike into your neighbor's flowerbed, confess and apologize. If a clerk gives you too much change back, return the extra money. You'll be building your honesty muscles!

IN YOUR FAITH COMMUNITY

★ Help teach younger members of your faith community about the importance of being honest. You could find religious stories or picture books about telling the truth and read them aloud. You could write a skit with other members of your youth group and perform it for the preschoolers. You could make a bulletin board like the one described on page 50 for your house of worship.

WITH YOUR FRIENDS

★ Make a pact not to lie to each other. You can do this with a handshake or with a more formal pledge that you put on paper. *Example:* "We promise to be honest with ourselves and each other. We pledge

to tell each other the truth, even when it's hard to do." Each of you should sign the pledge.

⭐ Take your pact or pledge seriously, but know that there are kind ways to be truthful. (That's known as *being tactful*.) So, if your friend asks, "How do you like my haircut?" and you think it looks awful, you don't have to say, "You look like you sat under a paper shredder!" Instead, put on your best smile and say, "Wow, you really went for a whole new look!"

Start Adding!

Pick at least ONE idea you've read here and give it a try. Then think about or write about what happened. Will you try another way to learn how to be more truthful and to make honesty an asset in your life?

Back to
Brianna's
Story

"Do you want to explain?" Brianna's dad says as they walk back home.

"Um, about what?"

"You know perfectly well what this is about: Your room. I went in there and it looked pretty much the same as it did yesterday—messy."

"Well, Daddy, maybe I'm not as good of a picker-upper as you are. I can't help that!"

Her dad stops and looks at her, disappointment written all over his face. Brianna wishes she could take back her words. She feels rotten.

Inside the house, her dad says, "Come on upstairs with me. I want to talk." He sits down on Brianna's partly-made bed, moving aside a pile of clothes.

"When I look around this room," he says quietly, "I don't just see a mess—I see a mess of lies you told me."

"I didn't lie about everything!" Brianna protests. "I cleaned up *some* stuff."

"Are you saying that you only lied a little, and so it's okay?"

Brianna looks away. "Dad, do you think we could start this day over?" she asks. "I mean, I'm really sorry, and I'm not going to lie anymore."

"Come over here," says her dad, pulling her close. "I forgive you. But no basketball this weekend."

Just then, something in Brianna's closet goes *thump thump CRASH.*

"*That* didn't sound good," says Brianna, smiling weakly.

"Neither do lies," says her father, standing up. "I'm glad to know I won't be hearing any more of those!"

Responsibility

What it means: Your parent(s) tell you it's important
to be responsible for your own behavior.

Erik's Story "Get back on your bike, David," Erik tells his five-year-old brother. "Spencer wants to come home with us and check out my soccer trophy."

Erik and Spencer start heading down the sidewalk on their bikes, but David doesn't budge. "I want to go to the park," he says, pouting.

"David, come *on!* My watch says it's time to go."

"Well, my watch says it's time to stay!"

"You don't even have a watch," Erik reminds his brother. Spencer rolls his eyes and snickers.

"Don't laugh!" David yells. He takes off his bike helmet and throws it on the ground.

55

"David, you're being a baby," says Erik angrily. "I let you ride with me today because you *said* you'd be good."

"I *am* good! And you're not the boss of me," his brother replies.

"I'm the boss when we're riding bikes. You're still on training wheels!"

When Spencer busts out laughing, Erik joins in. "David, this is your last chance," Erik warns. "We're going with you or without you."

David looks surprised. "You can't leave me here by myself!"

Erik grins. "Why not? You said I'm not the *boss* of you, right?"

David sits down on a patch of grass near the sidewalk. "Okay, then, go away," he says. "See if I care."

"Fine. We're out of here. Come on, Spencer," Erik says, leaving his brother behind.

Erik is learning about the *Responsibility* asset.

Think about your own life. Has a parent or another adult in your family talked to you about the importance of being responsible? Do you know that you're responsible for what you do and say? Do you admit your mistakes and try to make things better?

Facts!

Kids with the *Responsibility* asset:

✓ behave better in school

✓ have stronger social skills

✓ like themselves more

If **YES**, keep reading to learn ways to make this asset even stronger.

If **NO**, keep reading to learn ways to add this asset to your life.

You can also use these ideas to help add this asset for other people—like your friends, family members, neighbors, and kids at school.

 **AT HOME**

Make a List. Having responsibilities is a sign that you're getting older and learning how to handle more activities in your life. List your responsibilities on paper so you can see what they are. If you have a lot of them, you may need to break the list into groups like *school, chores, sports, lessons,* and so on. *Examples:* In the *lessons* group, your responsibilities might be to (1) attend the lesson (not skip it) and (2) practice several times during the week. For *sports,* you probably have to (1) go to practice, (2) go to meets, (3) show up on time, and (4) bring your gear.

Give Yourself Credit. When you look at your responsibilities list, you may be surprised at all you have to do. Put stars next to the responsibilities you're managing successfully. (This is a way to tell yourself, "Way to go!") Now look at the rest of your list. Are there a few responsibilities you could improve on? Choose one and make it your goal to pay more attention to that responsibility this week.

> **TIP:** At the end of the week, if you've met your goal, give yourself another star.

Ask Yourself How You're Doing. Think about your behavior at home. How is it? Pretty good? So-so? The pits? Signs that you're doing well might include more rights, fewer fights, and more privileges. Your parents trust you to make good choices, follow the rules, and do the right thing—in other words, to show *responsible* behavior. Signs that you're not doing so well might include . . . you probably already know. More fights, fewer privileges, and more consequences.

7 Super Ways to Show You're Responsible

1. When you make a promise, keep it.

2. Got chores? Do them now or as soon as you can. Don't *procrastinate* (put things off until later) or wait to be reminded.

3. Own up to your words and actions. Don't say "She made me do it!" or "It was your fault!" or "I couldn't help it!"

4. When in doubt, check it out. Not sure what's expected of you? Ask someone who knows.

5. Offer to take on more responsibilities as you get older.

6. If you mess up, 'fess up. Don't make excuses or play the blame game.

7. If you're going to be late coming home from a friend's house, pick up the phone and call.

Try a Little Harder. Talk to a family grown-up to get suggestions for positive changes. You may want to choose one problem area to work on first. *Example:* Maybe you're a little grumpy when you come home from school and you tend to raise your voice at your family. Think about *why* you might act that way. Are you riled up from the bus ride home? Worried about homework? Once you've identified the "why" behind your behavior, think of ways to change it. Maybe you need to do something physical the moment you get home so you can release energy. Or perhaps you could spend a half hour unwinding in a quiet place. Commit to doing things differently and see if your behavior improves. Chances are, it will.

 **AT SCHOOL**

★ Students who make excuses or play the blame game drive teachers crazy. Be a responsible student by doing your homework and assignments. Don't tell your teacher the dog ate your book report or your dad made you late for school—it hardly ever works. Besides, excuses and blaming are dishonest. Learn more about honesty on pages 45–54.

★ Use a day planner or keep a to-do list of your school assignments. Having a tool like this is a simple way to be more responsible.

★ Ask your teacher about other ways you can be more responsible in the classroom. See if he or she can give you some pointers on taking responsibility for what you say and for how you act.

IN YOUR NEIGHBORHOOD

★ You live there—and you can help make your neighborhood a better place. Take responsibility by picking up trash that's blowing along the curb or telling an adult about broken glass or graffiti you see at the playground or park. This will help make your community cleaner and safer for everyone.

★ Following rules is a great way to show that you're a responsible kid. *Examples:* If a sign reads "No skateboarding," find somewhere else to go. If you've got some gum wrappers or an empty drink bottle that you want to get rid of, wait until you find a trash can instead of littering. Wear your bike helmet when biking, scootering, or skating. Enough said!

IN YOUR FAITH COMMUNITY

★ Volunteer to help out before or after religious services. (Just make sure the grown-ups you ride with are willing to arrive early or stay late.) You may be able to get involved with clean-up, for example, or help your teacher prepare lessons. You could offer to help supervise activities for young children or lend a hand to an elderly or disabled person who needs assistance to stand or walk.

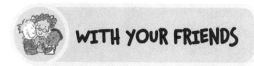

WITH YOUR FRIENDS

★ Respect each other's responsibilities. *Examples:* If you know your best friend has to do her chores every Saturday before playing outside, plan to wait until she's done. If you get an allowance for doing your chores but your friend doesn't, don't rub it in. If your friend babysits his younger sister after school, avoid making him feel like he's missing out on all the fun. (Maybe you could help him with the babysitting sometimes.)

★ Got a really dull and difficult chore? Ask a friend to help—and then offer to do a favor in return. Pulling weeds isn't a thrill, but it can be more fun if you and your friend play music while you work, take a lemonade break, and talk about your favorite Harry Potter book. The time will pass a lot more quickly!

Start Adding!

Pick at least ONE idea you've read here and give it a try. Then think about or write about what happened. Will you try another idea to improve your behavior and take more responsibility for what you do and say?

Back to
ERiK'S
Story

"Mom! Spencer's here to look at my trophy!" Erik yells as he comes in the front door.

"Sounds good," Erik's mom calls from the kitchen. "Send your brother in here, okay?"

"Hold on a sec, Spencer. You can go up to my room and look on my shelf. That's where the trophy is."

Erik goes into the kitchen where his mom is fixing dinner. "David refused to come home with us," he announces.

"What?!"

"I told him to come with me, but he wouldn't."

"Well, where is he?" she says, turning off the stove burners and looking worried.

"He's, like, a few blocks away," Erik says.

"Erik! He's only in kindergarten. He can't be left alone on the sidewalk or street somewhere! Please go get Spencer. We're all going to look for David."

Outside, his mom says anxiously, "Which way?"

"That way," Erik points. They all set off at a run. Suddenly Erik is worried, too. He thinks, "What if David wandered off or something and we can't find him? It'd be all my fault."

"There he is," Mom says with relief. Erik feels relieved, too, but then his stomach sinks. He wonders how much trouble he's in.

Mom hugs David as he wails, "They left me!"

She turns and gives Erik her serious look. "You're twelve. I trusted you to be in charge. David's okay, but he was probably really scared, and he could have gotten hurt."

"Mom," Erik starts to explain, "he wouldn't come—" Then he stops. He looks at Mom's tense face and David's tears.

"Whoa, I kind of blew it, didn't I?" Erik admits. "I shouldn't have left him alone. I was so excited to show Spencer my trophy, but that's no excuse." He pauses, then adds, "I'm really sorry— both of you."

Healthy Lifestyle

What it means: Your parent(s) tell you it's important to have good health habits and an understanding of healthy sexuality.

Zoe's Story

"Um, are you really sure we should do this?" Zoe asks her friend Mandy.

"Yeah! Come on, don't wimp out on me, okay?" Mandy holds the cigarette out to Zoe and she takes it, even though she's having major doubts.

"Where'd you get these, anyway?" Zoe asks.

"From that family I babysit for sometimes. They've got packs everywhere. They'll never notice."

"Great," Zoe thinks, "let's add getting caught stealing to the list of things to worry about!"

"Okay," Mandy says, turning the pages of the fashion magazine in front of them. She finds a cigarette ad and points to the model's hand. "See how she holds it all elegant like that? We have to copy her."

Zoe puts the cigarette between her fingers, trying to look experienced. "Like this?" she asks, angling her hand and striking a pose.

"Sort of, I guess. Here, let me light it for you." Mandy whips out a lighter and touches the flame to the end of Zoe's cigarette.

Nothing happens.

Zoe feels momentarily relieved. "It didn't light," she says.

"Here, let's try again," Mandy replies. "This time, breathe in really hard."

Zoe looks at Mandy, wanting to tell her to forget the whole stupid idea. But somehow, the words don't come.

Zoe thinks about her parents and all the warnings they've given her about cigarettes and drugs and alcohol. "What if they find out about this?" she wonders. But then she worries about what Mandy will think if she says no to smoking. Will she laugh at her? Will she tell the kids at school about Zoe the Chicken?

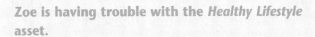

Zoe is having trouble with the *Healthy Lifestyle* asset.

Think about your own life. Do you have good health habits? Does your family? Do you take care of your body and avoid substances that could harm it? Has a family adult warned you about risks to your health? Are the adults at home comfortable talking with you about sex?

If **YES,** keep reading to learn ways to make this asset even stronger.

Facts!

Kids with the *Healthy Lifestyle* asset:

✔ do better in school

✔ eat more fruits and veggies

✔ are less likely to use cigarettes, alcohol, and other drugs

If **NO,** keep reading to learn ways to add this asset to your life.

You can also use these ideas to help add this asset for other people—like your friends, family members, neighbors, and kids at school.

 **AT HOME**

Use Your Feet. That's what they're there for! Human beings are built for walking—but most of us don't do enough of it. How about *your* family? Do you exercise together? Take walks around the neighborhood? Go

on long hikes on weekends? Or take the stairs at the mall instead of using escalators or elevators? Each of these activities increases the number of steps you and your family take every day—and that means you're all healthier. Experts suggest aiming for 10,000 steps a day (that's a lot!). If your dad or mom tends to be a couch potato or often says, "I don't have time for exercise," you can remind him or her about the importance of being active.

Challenge Yourself to Be Healthier. Exercise, eat right, take care of yourself . . . you've probably heard all this before. Well, it's good advice. You'll feel better if you take care of your body (a positive value you can work toward all your life). One way to get inspired is to look for a role model in your family—someone who inspires you to stay healthy. Maybe you have a cousin who's an awesome hockey player, or perhaps your grandma is still active enough to kick a ball with you in the yard. Talk to this person about ways you can stay healthy and fit.

A message for you:

For some kids, home isn't a very healthy place to be. Maybe the grown-ups there smoke, use drugs, or drink a lot of alcohol. Maybe they don't eat healthy foods, they're overweight, or they hardly ever exercise. If your home seems unhealthy or unhappy to you, try to spend more time in positive places. Look for adults you can trust and ask for help. *Examples:* Sign up for after-school activities or community programs for kids—especially ones that include sports or outdoor games. Hang out at friends' homes where people respect their bodies and make good choices about their health. Get to know neighbors who are good role models.

Don't Be Tempted. Taking care of yourself includes avoiding harmful activities like smoking or experimenting with alcohol or other drugs. Now that you're getting older, other kids or teens might pressure you to try this unhealthy stuff (or you might just be curious to see what it's like). You probably know these activities are against the law for someone your age. But do you know that they are a major risk to your health? Your health is the most valuable thing you have! (It ranks right up there with your family.) And speaking of your family, they can be a great resource for you. If you're feeling pressured or curious about smoking, for instance, talk to a family adult you trust. *Example:* "Uncle Ed, I've heard that other kids my age have tried smoking. Sometimes, I get the feeling I'm the only one who hasn't tried it. What should I do?" *X-treme example:* "Mom, I have to tell you something, but I think you'll be mad. I tried some beer when I spent the night at Robin's. I feel really bad about it, and I'm sorry. Can we talk about it?" Reaching out to a trusted adult is an important way to get help with the Healthy Lifestyle asset.

Watch What You Watch. Next time you're watching a kids' TV show, count how many commercials you see for junk foods like potato chips, sugared cereal, cookies, fast food, soda, candy, and so on. Pay special attention to ads for foods that *sound* good for you, even when they're not. You know the ones: sugary yogurt that comes in a tube, fruit-flavored drinks that aren't really juice, sugar-coated cereal, or prepackaged lunches that contain fatty meats and cheeses. Often, the ads talk about how these foods are easy for kids "on the go" or are "part of a balanced meal." Try to limit foods like these. You may even decide to turn off the TV so you don't have to watch the ads.

Enjoy Being a Kid. Do you think a lot about the future—the days when you'll be an older teen or an adult? It probably seems like you'll *finally* get to do all kinds of cool things that aren't possible for you right now (like driving, wearing whatever you want, having more money to spend, and being free to make all your own choices). And sometimes, it might be tempting to try to get to that point faster, maybe by dressing in a more grown-up style or by trying to do things that seem more adult. That pull toward adulthood can feel confusing. Just know one thing: It's great to be a kid! Don't feel the pressure to grow up too fast. Keep reading picture books, pretending, singing when you feel like it, acting silly, and playing with your younger siblings. Daydream. Watch the clouds drift by. Enjoy every moment of being young.

Ask Questions. Body changes, crushes, s-e-x . . . all these things bring up *a lot* of questions. And it's normal to feel like the questions are too weird or embarrassing to ask. In fact, *no question is a dumb question.* And how will you learn the answers if you don't speak up? Today, decide on at least one family adult you trust enough to ask even the most embarrassing question. Get up your courage and then say, "I have a question about something. Can I ask you, please?" Once you open that door, it will be easier to ask the next time.

Ewwwwww Gross!

Do your parents kiss right in front of you? Do they hold hands when you're out in public together, like in a restaurant or at the mall? Do you often hear them say "I love you" to each other?

If you can answer **YES** to one or more of these questions, you're lucky.

You may be thinking, "WHAT? That's gross!" But think about it: Those Public Displays of Affection (PDAs) show that your parents care for each other. And even if it makes you a little uncomfortable (especially in public), you're learning something important about healthy adult relationships. Years from now, you might actually feel like it was kind of cool to grow up with parents who showed affection. That kind of role modeling can teach you how to be a more loving, caring person.

Note: If your parents don't fit this profile, you can still learn about healthy adult relationships from other sources. What about other trusted grownups—stepparents, foster parents, grandparents, or aunts and uncles?

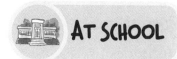

AT SCHOOL

★ All kids used to have both recess and gym at school. (Just ask your parents or grandparents.) If you do, don't complain. Physical activity releases pent-up energy, builds your strength, and increases your brainpower—all good things you need every day. *P.S.* Put some muscle into those physical activities. Don't just talk during recess or pretend to do your push-ups in Phy. Ed. It's good to break a sweat.

★ If you're not already on a sports team, join one. Or try out for a new sport in addition to the one you already play. Maybe you need a new challenge!

★ Do your best to eat a healthy lunch at school. If you pack a lunch every day, try to include at least one fruit or vegetable (carrot sticks, an apple, or raisins). If you buy lunch, don't ignore the healthy stuff. Drink water or milk instead of soda. And definitely avoid skipping lunch. Food provides the energy you need to get through the day.

IN YOUR NEIGHBORHOOD

⭐ Take l-o-o-o-n-g walks—remember, you're working toward 10,000 steps per day. Walk your dog more than once each day. (If you don't have a dog, you might offer to walk a neighbor's.) Take an after-dinner walk with your family a few times each week or more.

⭐ Maybe you see some of the kids and teens who live near you smoking cigarettes or using chewing tobacco. Maybe they've tried to get you to do what they do. It can be hard to resist the pressure, but it's easier if you know why you should stay away from these substances. The why is simple: Because you value your body, your mind, and your health.

> **TIP:** What can you say when someone pressures you? Try "No," "No, thanks," "Nope," "No way," "Uh-uh," "Forget it," "I'm not interested," "I don't want to," or "My parents would ground me for life." Then walk away.

⭐ Learn what your religious tradition teaches about the use of alcohol and drugs, and about sexuality. You may feel the most comfortable talking about these issues with the adults in your family, or you may prefer to reach out to your religious leader or teacher instead. Ask questions. Get the support and the information you need to stay healthy.

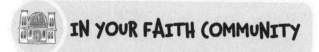

IN YOUR FAITH COMMUNITY

★ Talk to your religion teacher about having the kids in your class make a pledge to take good care of their health and avoid risky behaviors. You may want to write the pledge on a small card that you can carry with you in your pocket or backpack. The card will remind you of the promise you've made.

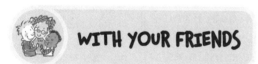

WITH YOUR FRIENDS

★ When you get together with friends, go outdoors, walk in the park, or head to the nearest playground. If you don't have a bike or in-line skates, how about a jump rope? Or a ball you can throw back and forth? No equipment? Just run and do cartwheels and chase each other around. The important thing is to get moving.

★ Talk to your friends about your commitment to take care of yourself. If they pressure you to do harmful things like smoke, go on a crash diet, or experiment with drugs or sex, know that you don't have to give in.

★ You and your friends can role-play saying no. That way, if you are ever pressured, you'll know just what line to use. Practice the words over and over so you can say them without laughing or losing confidence.

Start Adding!

Pick at least ONE idea you've read here and give it a try. Then think about or write about what happened. Will you try another way to practice good health habits and stay true to your values?

Back to
Zoe's
Story Zoe wonders which would feel worse: getting yelled at by her parents (if they learn about the smoking) or getting laughed at by her friend (if she refuses to light up). "There's a chance Mom and Dad will never find out about this," she thinks, "but Mandy will definitely know if I wimp out."

"Okay, I'm ready," Zoe decides, holding the cigarette to her lips.

"Cool," Mandy says, smiling. As Mandy lights the cigarette, Zoe takes a deep breath. Suddenly her throat feels like it's on fire. She coughs—*hard*—and starts to choke. The smoke surrounds her, and she quickly tosses the burning cigarette on the ground. Her eyes sting. It takes her a moment to catch her breath.

Mandy collapses in a fit of laughter. "You should have seen your face!" she says. "You didn't look like the model *at all*. You looked like . . . like you just ate some really bad cafeteria food!"

"Oh, you think you're so hilarious, don't you!" Zoe replies.

"What?" Mandy says, acting innocent.

She gets up and brushes off her jeans. "Come on, can't you take a joke?"

"Some joke! First, you made me smoke, which for your information, I didn't even want to do. If you're so cool, why don't *you* do it? And when I started choking, you acted like it was the funniest thing ever!"

Mandy looks at her evenly. "Nobody made you do anything. You decided."

Zoe looks at her friend and feels tears of anger welling up. She realizes she's not just mad at Mandy but at herself, too.

"I'm going home, Mandy. And just so you know, I'm going to tell my parents what we did."

"No way!"

"Yeah, I am. They deserve to know," she says, heading home.

Moments later, she hears Mandy's voice in the distance, yelling, "Wait up!"

Mandy runs to her and says, "I'm sorry. I was a jerk."

"Yeah, you were," Zoe agrees. Then she smiles, "We *both* were, and trying to smoke was a really stupid thing to do. Come on, let's go."

A NOTE TO GROWN-UPS

Ongoing research by Search Institute, a nonprofit organization based in Minneapolis, Minnesota, shows that young people who succeed have specific assets in their lives— **Developmental Assets** including family support, a caring neighborhood, integrity, resistance skills, self-esteem, and a sense of purpose. This book, along with the other seven books in the **Adding Assets Series for Kids**, empowers young people ages 8–12 to build their own Developmental Assets.

But it's very important to acknowledge that building assets for and with young people is primarily an *adult* responsibility. What kids need most in their lives are grown-ups—parents and other relatives, teachers, school administrators, neighbors, youth leaders, religious leaders, community members, policy makers, advocates, and more—who care about them as individuals. They need adults who care enough to learn their names, to show interest in their lives, to listen when they talk, to provide them with opportunities to realize their potential, to teach them well, to give them sound advice, to serve as good examples, to guide them, to inspire them, to support them when they stumble, and to shield them from harm—as much as is humanly possible these days.

This book focuses on six of the 40 Developmental Assets identified by Search Institute. These are **Internal Assets**—values, skills, and self-perceptions that kids develop *internally*, with your help. The internal assets described here are called the **Positive Values Assets**. They're about forming the beliefs and convictions that will guide one's choices and behaviors throughout life. While all 40 assets support character development, these are the "character assets." They determine the kind of adult the child will one day become.

The role of adults (especially parents) in asset-building is underscored by how the six Positive Values assets are defined for children in middle childhood. Each definition begins with these words: "Parent(s) tell the child it is important to . . . ." For children this age, values are still evolving. Their behaviors may change from day to day, or from one situation to the next, which is why we don't think of these children as "having" values—not yet, at least. Much of what your children eventually believe about honesty, equality and social justice, integrity, responsibility, caring, and a healthy lifestyle will come from you. Your words and actions are laying the groundwork for their character.

A list of all 40 Developmental Assets for middle childhood, with definitions, follows. If you want to know more about the assets, some of the resources listed on pages 86–87 will help you. Or you can visit the Search Institute Web site at *www.search-institute.org.*

Thank you for caring enough about kids to make this book available to the young person or persons in your life. We'd love to hear your success stories, and we welcome your suggestions for adding assets to kids' lives—or improving future editions of this book.

Pamela Espeland and Elizabeth Verdick
Free Spirit Publishing Inc.
217 Fifth Avenue North, Suite 200
Minneapolis, MN 55401-1299
help4kids@freespirit.com

The 40 Developmental Assets for Middle Childhood

EXTERNAL ASSETS

SUPPORT

1. **Family support**—Family life provides high levels of love and support.
2. **Positive family communication**—Parent(s) and child communicate positively. Child feels comfortable seeking advice and counsel from parent(s).
3. **Other adult relationships**—Child receives support from adults other than her or his parent(s).
4. **Caring neighborhood**—Child experiences caring neighbors.
5. **Caring school climate**—Relationships with teachers and peers provide a caring, encouraging school environment.
6. **Parent involvement in schooling**—Parent(s) are actively involved in helping the child succeed in school.

EMPOWERMENT

7. **Community values children**—Child feels valued and appreciated by adults in the community.
8. **Children as resources**—Child is included in decisions at home and in the community.
9. **Service to others**—Child has opportunities to help others in the community.
10. **Safety**—Child feels safe at home, at school, and in her or his neighborhood.

BOUNDARIES AND EXPECTATIONS

11. **Family boundaries**—Family has clear and consistent rules and consequences and monitors the child's whereabouts.
12. **School boundaries**—School provides clear rules and consequences.
13. **Neighborhood boundaries**—Neighbors take responsibility for monitoring the child's behavior.
14. **Adult role models**—Parents(s) and other adults in the child's family, as well as nonfamily adults, model positive, responsible behavior.
15. **Positive peer influence**—Child's closest friends model positive, responsible behavior.
16. **High expectations**—Parent(s) and teachers expect the child to do her or his best at school and in other activities.

CONSTRUCTIVE USE OF TIME

17. **Creative activities**—Child participates in music, art, drama, or creative writing two or more times per week.
18. **Child programs**—Child participates two or more times per week in cocurricular school activities or structured community programs for children.
19. **Religious community**—Child attends religious programs or services one or more times per week.
20. **Time at home**—Child spends some time most days both in high-quality interaction with parent(s) and doing things at home other than watching TV or playing video games.

INTERNAL ASSETS

COMMITMENT TO LEARNING

21. **Achievement motivation**—Child is motivated and strives to do well in school.
22. **Learning engagement**—Child is responsive, attentive, and actively engaged in learning at school and enjoys participating in learning activities outside of school.
23. **Homework**—Child usually hands in homework on time.
24. **Bonding to adults at school**—Child cares about teachers and other adults at school.
25. **Reading for pleasure**—Child enjoys and engages in reading for fun most days of the week.

POSITIVE VALUES

26. **Caring**—Parent(s) tell the child it is important to help other people.
27. **Equality and social justice**—Parent(s) tell the child it is important to speak up for equal rights for all people.
28. **Integrity**—Parent(s) tell the child it is important to stand up for one's beliefs.
29. **Honesty**—Parent(s) tell the child it is important to tell the truth.
30. **Responsibility**—Parent(s) tell the child it is important to accept personal responsibility for behavior.
31. **Healthy lifestyle**—Parent(s) tell the child it is important to have good health habits and an understanding of healthy sexuality.

SOCIAL COMPETENCIES

32. **Planning and decision making**—Child thinks about decisions and is usually happy with the results of her or his decisions.
33. **Interpersonal competence**—Child cares about and is affected by other people's feelings, enjoys making friends, and, when frustrated or angry, tries to calm herself or himself.
34. **Cultural competence**—Child knows and is comfortable with people of different racial, ethnic, and cultural backgrounds and with her or his own cultural identity.
35. **Resistance skills**—Child can stay away from people who are likely to get her or him in trouble and is able to say no to doing wrong or dangerous things.
36. **Peaceful conflict resolution**—Child attempts to resolve conflict nonviolently.

POSITIVE IDENTITY

37. **Personal power**—Child feels he or she has some influence over things that happen in her or his life.
38. **Self-esteem**—Child likes and is proud to be the person he or she is.
39. **Sense of purpose**—Child sometimes thinks about what life means and whether there is a purpose for her or his life.
40. **Positive view of personal future**—Child is optimistic about her or his personal future.

Helpful Resources

Books

Don't Tell a Whopper on Fridays! The Children's Truth-Control Book by Adolph Moser (Kansas City, MO: Landmark Editions, 1999). Sometimes telling the truth is hard and lying seems a lot easier. This book covers the problems of lying and the importance of telling the truth. It gives examples you can relate to and ideas that will help you tell the truth, even when it's hard.

If You Had to Choose, What Would You Do? by Sandra McLeod Humphrey (Amherst, NY: Prometheus Books, 2003). Is it wrong to sneak into the movies if your big brother says it's okay? If "everybody" is cheating on the math test, shouldn't you, too? Read 25 real-life situations, then think about what you would do. **Tip:** If you like this book, you can look for two more books by this author: *More If You Had to Choose, What Would You Do* and *It's Up to You . . . What Do You Do?*

Judge Judy Sheindlin's Win or Lose by How You Choose! by Judge Judy Sheindlin (New York: HarperCollins, 2000). This book asks you to decide what's best to do in all kinds of situations. Can you make the right decision? How can you know for sure? Share this book with your parents or other family grown-ups and talk about the issues.

Think for Yourself: A Kid's Guide to Solving Life's Dilemmas and Other Sticky Problems by Cynthia MacGregor (Toronto: Lobster Press, 2003). This book breaks down daily problems into categories: friends, family, grown-ups, and everyday situations. Real-life examples and choices for solutions help you learn to think things through and make good decisions.

Web sites

Too Smart to Start
www.toosmarttostart.samhsa.gov/youth.html
Are you smart enough NOT to start using alcohol or other drugs? Read advice from teens about how and why to say no. Do crossword puzzles and word searches. Tell your parents or other family adults about this Web site; there's good stuff here for grown-ups, too.

Youth as Resources
www.yar.org
Kids really can make a difference. YAR supports youth-led service projects, from juvenile justice to public housing and any issue that motivates kids to make our world a better place. Find a YAR program near you, or start your own.

Youth Service America
www.servenet.org
Connect to organizations and service projects in your area. Type in your ZIP code, skills, and interests to find the best experience for you.

Books

Building Assets Is Elementary: Group Activities for Helping Kids Ages 8–12 Succeed by Search Institute (Minneapolis: Search Institute, 2004). Promoting creativity, time-management skills, kindness, manners, and more, this flexible activity book includes over 50 easy-to-use group exercises for the classroom or youth group.

Character Building Activities for Kids: Ready-to-Use Character Education Lessons & Activities for the Elementary Grades by Darlene Mannix (San Francisco: Jossey-Bass, 2002). Includes more than 140 lessons (with reproducibles) for developing character traits such as honesty, generosity, and fairness.

Character Matters: How to Help Our Children Develop Good Judgment, Integrity, and Other Essential Virtues by Thomas Lickona (New York: Touchstone, 2004). An award-winning psychologist offers more than 100 practical strategies for helping kids build strong personal character.

10-Minute Life Lessons for Kids: 52 Fun and Simple Games and Activities to Teach Your Child Honesty, Trust, Love, and Other Important Values by Jamie C. Miller (New York: HarperCollins, 1998). Playful, easy-to-understand activities help parents teach children moral lessons they won't forget.

What Kids Need to Succeed: Proven, Practical Ways to Raise Good Kids by Peter L. Benson, Ph.D., Judy Galbraith, M.A., and Pamela Espeland (Minneapolis: Free Spirit Publishing, 1994). More than 900 specific, concrete suggestions help adults help children build Developmental Assets at home, at school, and in the community.

What Young Children Need to Succeed: Working Together to Build Assets from Birth to Age 11 by Jolene L. Roehlkepartain and Nancy Leffert, Ph.D. (Minneapolis: Free Spirit Publishing,

2000). Hundreds of practical, concrete ideas help adults build Developmental Assets for children in four different age groups: birth to 12 months, ages 1–2, 3–5, and 6–11. Includes inspiring true stories from across the United States.

Web sites

Center for the 4th & 5th Rs (Respect & Responsibility)
www.cortland.edu/character/index.asp
A regional, state, and national resource in character education, founded by Dr. Thomas Lickona. Subscribe to the free online newsletter.

Children Lead
www.childrenlead.com
A division of LeadershipVillage.com, this site offers daily tips and informative articles about parenting for character and leadership.

The Giraffe Project
www.giraffe.org
The Giraffe Project works to inspire K–12 students to be courageous, active citizens. Their site includes helpful resources and extraordinary stories about heroes of all ages who are willing to stick out their necks to help others.

GoodCharacter.com
www.goodcharacter.com
Discussion questions, learning activities, writing assignments, and other useful resources for educators. Recommended by the Parents' Choice Foundation.

Search Institute
www.search-institute.org
Through dynamic research and analysis, this independent nonprofit organization works to promote healthy, active, and content youth and communities.

Index

A

Adults
  healthy relationships among, 73
  message to, 80–81
  showing appreciation to, 8–9
  talking to, 11, 70, 71, 72, 75–76
  unhealthy lifestyles of, 70
Alcohol, 70, 75–76
Amnesty International (AI), 29
Appreciation, showing
  to adults, 8–9
  for freedoms, 25–26
  to friends, 15
  to younger children, 40
Assets. *See* Developmental assets

B

Blame game, 59, 60
Body changes, questions about, 72
Bullying, 27, 28, 30

C

Caring asset
  described, 2, 6
  effects of having, 8
  example of, 6–7, 17–19
  ways to add
    in faith community, 14
    with friends, 15–16
    at home, 8–11
    in neighborhood, 13–14
    at school, 11–12
Choices, 3
Conscience, 1

D

Developmental assets
  described, 1–2
  external, 82
  importance of, 3
  internal, 80, 83
Dishonesty
  effects of, 47–48
  excuses and, 59, 60
  in neighborhood, 50
Drugs, using, 70, 75–76

E

Empathy, described, 9
Equality and social justice asset
  described, 2, 20
  effects of having, 22
  example of, 20–21, 31–32
  ways to add
    in faith community, 29
    with friends, 30
    at home, 22–27
    in neighborhood, 28
    at school, 27–28
Excuses, making, 59, 60
External assets, described, 82

F

Faith community
  helping out in, 14, 62
  learning about integrity in, 40–41
  promoting equality and social
    justice in, 29
  promoting healthy lifestyle in, 76
  promoting honesty in, 51

traditions about substance
    use, 75–76
Families
    being caring in, 8–11
    exercising with, 68–69
    handling responsibilities in, 57–59
    honesty in, 47–49, 59
    kinds of, 5
    photographs of, 37
    role models in, 36, 69
    values of, 24–25
Feelings, about equality, 26–27
Freedoms, appreciating, 25–26
Friends
    being honest with, 51–52
    helping, 63
    integrity of, 41
    loyalty to, 30, 35–36
    making neighborhood, 28
    promoting healthy lifestyle
        with, 76–77
    respecting responsibilities
        of, 62–63
    showing appreciation to, 15
    volunteering with, 16

G

Giraffe Heroes Project, 12
Grown-ups. See adults

H

Healthy lifestyle asset
    described, 2, 66
    effects of having, 68
    example of, 66–67, 78–79
    ways to add
        in faith community, 76
        with friends, 76–77

at home, 68–73
    in neighborhood, 75–76
    at school, 74
Honesty asset
    described, 2, 45
    effects of having, 47
    example of, 45–46, 53–54
    ways to add
        in faith community, 51
        with friends, 51–52
        at home, 47–49
        in neighborhood, 50
        at school, 50
Human rights, 24, 29

I

I Believe lists, 22–23
Integrity, described, 36
Integrity asset
    described, 2, 33
    effects of having, 35
    example of, 33–34, 43–44
    ways to add
        in faith community, 40–41
        with friends, 41
        at home, 35–38
        in neighborhood, 39–40
        at school, 38–39
Internal assets, described, 80, 83

J

Junk foods, 71

K

Kids Care Clubs, 15
Kindness, acts of, 9–10

L

Loyalty, 30, 35–38
Lying. *See* dishonesty

M

Morals, 1

N

Neighborhood
    being responsible in, 61–62
    bullying and teasing in, 28
    exercise programs in, 70
    healthy lifestyle in, 75–76
    helping out in, 13–14
    making friends in, 28
    promoting honesty in, 50
    role models in, 39–40, 70

P

Parents, note about, 5
Parks, Rosa, 36
Peer pressure, 75, 77
Photographs, 37, 41
Pledge cards, 51–52, 76
Points of Light Foundation, 12–13
Positive values assets, 1–2, 80–81
Prisoners of Conscience (POCs), 29
Procrastination, 59
Public Displays of Affection (PDAs), 73

R

Responsibility asset
    described, 2, 55
    effects of having, 57
    example of, 55–56, 64–65
    ways to add
        in faith community, 62

    with friends, 62–63
    at home, 57–60
    in neighborhood, 61–62
    at school, 60–61
Role models
    in family, 36, 69
    finding, 12–13
    in neighborhood, 39–40, 70
    at school, 38–39

S

School
    being responsible at, 60–61
    bullying and teasing at, 27–38
    eating at, 74
    physical activity at, 70, 74
    promoting honesty at, 50
    role models at, 38–39
    service clubs at, 11–12
Service clubs, 11–12, 15
Sexuality, questions about, 72
Smoking, 70–71, 75
Social justice, described, 25
Social justice asset. *See* equality and
    social justice asset

T

Teasing, 28, 30
Truthfulness, 48–49, 52

U

Universal Declaration of Human
    Rights, 24

V

Values, listing, 22–23
Volunteering, 10–11, 16, 62

About the Authors

Both Pamela Espeland and Elizabeth Verdick have written many books for children and teens.

Pamela is the coauthor (with Peter L. Benson and Judy Galbraith) of *What Kids Need to Succeed* and *What Teens Need to Succeed* and the author of *Succeed Every Day,* all based on Search Institute's concept of the 40 Developmental Assets. She is the author of *Life Lists for Teens* and the coauthor (with Gershen Kaufman and Lev Raphael) of *Stick Up for Yourself!*

Elizabeth is a children's book writer and editor. She is the author of *Germs Are Not for Sharing, Tails Are Not for Pulling, Teeth Are Not for Biting, Words Are Not for Hurting,* and *Feet Are Not for Kicking,* and coauthor (with Marjorie Lisovskis) of *How to Take the GRRRR Out of Anger* and (with Trevor Romain) of *Stress Can Really Get on Your Nerves* and *True or False? Tests Stink!*

Pamela and Elizabeth first worked together on *Making Every Day Count.* They live in Minnesota with their families and pets.

More Titles in the Adding Assets Series for Kids

To order, call **1.800.735.7323** or visit ***www.freespirit.com***

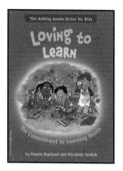

Each book is for ages 8–12.

Each 80–100 pp.; $9.95; softcover; two-color illust.; 5⅛" x 7".

www.freespirit.com